These Passwords Belong To:

_____

_____

_____

_____

A

NAME:

SITE:

USERNAME:

PASSWORD:

NOTES:

NAME:

SITE:

USERNAME:

PASSWORD:

NOTES:

NAME:

SITE:

USERNAME:

PASSWORD:

NOTES:

A

NAME:

SITE:

USERNAME:

PASSWORD:

NOTES:

NAME:

SITE:

USERNAME:

PASSWORD:

NOTES:

NAME:

SITE:

USERNAME:

PASSWORD:

NOTES:

A

NAME:

SITE:

USERNAME:

PASSWORD:

NOTES:

NAME:

SITE:

USERNAME:

PASSWORD:

NOTES:

NAME:

SITE:

USERNAME:

PASSWORD:

NOTES:

A

NAME:

SITE:

USERNAME:

PASSWORD:

NOTES:

NAME:

SITE:

USERNAME:

PASSWORD:

NOTES:

NAME:

SITE:

USERNAME:

PASSWORD:

NOTES:

B

NAME:

SITE:

USERNAME:

PASSWORD:

NOTES:

NAME:

SITE:

USERNAME:

PASSWORD:

NOTES:

NAME:

SITE:

USERNAME:

PASSWORD:

NOTES:

NAME:

SITE:

USERNAME:

PASSWORD:

NOTES:

NAME:

SITE:

USERNAME:

PASSWORD:

NOTES:

NAME:

SITE:

USERNAME:

PASSWORD:

NOTES:

B

NAME: _____

SITE: _____

USERNAME: _____

PASSWORD: _____

NOTES: _____

_____

NAME: _____

SITE: _____

USERNAME: _____

PASSWORD: _____

NOTES: _____

_____

NAME: _____

SITE: _____

USERNAME: _____

PASSWORD: _____

NOTES: _____

_____

NAME:

SITE:

USERNAME:

PASSWORD:

NOTES:

NAME:

SITE:

USERNAME:

PASSWORD:

NOTES:

NAME:

SITE:

USERNAME:

PASSWORD:

NOTES:

C

NAME:

SITE:

USERNAME:

PASSWORD:

NOTES:

NAME:

SITE:

USERNAME:

PASSWORD:

NOTES:

NAME:

SITE:

USERNAME:

PASSWORD:

NOTES:

C

NAME:

SITE:

USERNAME:

PASSWORD:

NOTES:

NAME:

SITE:

USERNAME:

PASSWORD:

NOTES:

NAME:

SITE:

USERNAME:

PASSWORD:

NOTES:

C

NAME:

SITE:

USERNAME:

PASSWORD:

NOTES:

NAME:

SITE:

USERNAME:

PASSWORD:

NOTES:

NAME:

SITE:

USERNAME:

PASSWORD:

NOTES:

C

NAME:

SITE:

USERNAME:

PASSWORD:

NOTES:

NAME:

SITE:

USERNAME:

PASSWORD:

NOTES:

NAME:

SITE:

USERNAME:

PASSWORD:

NOTES:

D

NAME:

SITE:

USERNAME:

PASSWORD:

NOTES:

NAME:

SITE:

USERNAME:

PASSWORD:

NOTES:

NAME:

SITE:

USERNAME:

PASSWORD:

NOTES:

D

NAME:

SITE:

USERNAME:

PASSWORD:

NOTES:

NAME:

SITE:

USERNAME:

PASSWORD:

NOTES:

NAME:

SITE:

USERNAME:

PASSWORD:

NOTES:

D

NAME:

SITE:

USERNAME:

PASSWORD:

NOTES:

NAME:

SITE:

USERNAME:

PASSWORD:

NOTES:

NAME:

SITE:

USERNAME:

PASSWORD:

NOTES:

D

NAME:

SITE:

USERNAME:

PASSWORD:

NOTES:

NAME:

SITE:

USERNAME:

PASSWORD:

NOTES:

NAME:

SITE:

USERNAME:

PASSWORD:

NOTES:

E

NAME:

SITE:

USERNAME:

PASSWORD:

NOTES:

NAME:

SITE:

USERNAME:

PASSWORD:

NOTES:

NAME:

SITE:

USERNAME:

PASSWORD:

NOTES:

E

NAME:

SITE:

USERNAME:

PASSWORD:

NOTES:

NAME:

SITE:

USERNAME:

PASSWORD:

NOTES:

NAME:

SITE:

USERNAME:

PASSWORD:

NOTES:

E

NAME:

SITE:

USERNAME:

PASSWORD:

NOTES:

NAME:

SITE:

USERNAME:

PASSWORD:

NOTES:

NAME:

SITE:

USERNAME:

PASSWORD:

NOTES:

E

NAME:

SITE:

USERNAME:

PASSWORD:

NOTES:

NAME:

SITE:

USERNAME:

PASSWORD:

NOTES:

NAME:

SITE:

USERNAME:

PASSWORD:

NOTES:

F

NAME:

SITE:

USERNAME:

PASSWORD:

NOTES:

NAME:

SITE:

USERNAME:

PASSWORD:

NOTES:

NAME:

SITE:

USERNAME:

PASSWORD:

NOTES:

F

NAME:

SITE:

USERNAME:

PASSWORD:

NOTES:

NAME:

SITE:

USERNAME:

PASSWORD:

NOTES:

NAME:

SITE:

USERNAME:

PASSWORD:

NOTES:

F

NAME:

SITE:

USERNAME:

PASSWORD:

NOTES:

NAME:

SITE:

USERNAME:

PASSWORD:

NOTES:

NAME:

SITE:

USERNAME:

PASSWORD:

NOTES:

F

NAME:

SITE:

USERNAME:

PASSWORD:

NOTES:

NAME:

SITE:

USERNAME:

PASSWORD:

NOTES:

NAME:

SITE:

USERNAME:

PASSWORD:

NOTES:

G

NAME:

SITE:

USERNAME:

PASSWORD:

NOTES:

NAME:

SITE:

USERNAME:

PASSWORD:

NOTES:

NAME:

SITE:

USERNAME:

PASSWORD:

NOTES:

NAME:

SITE:

USERNAME:

PASSWORD:

NOTES:

NAME:

SITE:

USERNAME:

PASSWORD:

NOTES:

NAME:

SITE:

USERNAME:

PASSWORD:

NOTES:

G

NAME:

SITE:

USERNAME:

PASSWORD:

NOTES:

NAME:

SITE:

USERNAME:

PASSWORD:

NOTES:

NAME:

SITE:

USERNAME:

PASSWORD:

NOTES:

G

NAME:

SITE:

USERNAME:

PASSWORD:

NOTES:

NAME:

SITE:

USERNAME:

PASSWORD:

NOTES:

NAME:

SITE:

USERNAME:

PASSWORD:

NOTES:

H

NAME:

SITE:

USERNAME:

PASSWORD:

NOTES:

NAME:

SITE:

USERNAME:

PASSWORD:

NOTES:

NAME:

SITE:

USERNAME:

PASSWORD:

NOTES:

H

NAME:

SITE:

USERNAME:

PASSWORD:

NOTES:

NAME:

SITE:

USERNAME:

PASSWORD:

NOTES:

NAME:

SITE:

USERNAME:

PASSWORD:

NOTES:

H

NAME:

SITE:

USERNAME:

PASSWORD:

NOTES:

NAME:

SITE:

USERNAME:

PASSWORD:

NOTES:

NAME:

SITE:

USERNAME:

PASSWORD:

NOTES:

NAME:

SITE:

USERNAME:

PASSWORD:

NOTES:

NAME:

SITE:

USERNAME:

PASSWORD:

NOTES:

NAME:

SITE:

USERNAME:

PASSWORD:

NOTES:

I

NAME:

SITE:

USERNAME:

PASSWORD:

NOTES:

NAME:

SITE:

USERNAME:

PASSWORD:

NOTES:

NAME:

SITE:

USERNAME:

PASSWORD:

NOTES:

NAME:

SITE:

USERNAME:

PASSWORD:

NOTES:

NAME:

SITE:

USERNAME:

PASSWORD:

NOTES:

NAME:

SITE:

USERNAME:

PASSWORD:

NOTES:

I

NAME:

SITE:

USERNAME:

PASSWORD:

NOTES:

NAME:

SITE:

USERNAME:

PASSWORD:

NOTES:

NAME:

SITE:

USERNAME:

PASSWORD:

NOTES:

NAME:

SITE:

USERNAME:

PASSWORD:

NOTES:

NAME:

SITE:

USERNAME:

PASSWORD:

NOTES:

NAME:

SITE:

USERNAME:

PASSWORD:

NOTES:

J

NAME:

SITE:

USERNAME:

PASSWORD:

NOTES:

NAME:

SITE:

USERNAME:

PASSWORD:

NOTES:

NAME:

SITE:

USERNAME:

PASSWORD:

NOTES:

NAME:

SITE:

USERNAME:

PASSWORD:

NOTES:

NAME:

SITE:

USERNAME:

PASSWORD:

NOTES:

NAME:

SITE:

USERNAME:

PASSWORD:

NOTES:

J

NAME:

SITE:

USERNAME:

PASSWORD:

NOTES:

~~~~~~

NAME:

SITE:

USERNAME:

PASSWORD:

NOTES:

~~~~~~

NAME:

SITE:

USERNAME:

PASSWORD:

NOTES:

J

NAME:

SITE:

USERNAME:

PASSWORD:

NOTES:

NAME:

SITE:

USERNAME:

PASSWORD:

NOTES:

NAME:

SITE:

USERNAME:

PASSWORD:

NOTES:

K

NAME:

SITE:

USERNAME:

PASSWORD:

NOTES:

NAME:

SITE:

USERNAME:

PASSWORD:

NOTES:

NAME:

SITE:

USERNAME:

PASSWORD:

NOTES:

K

NAME:

SITE:

USERNAME:

PASSWORD:

NOTES:

NAME:

SITE:

USERNAME:

PASSWORD:

NOTES:

NAME:

SITE:

USERNAME:

PASSWORD:

NOTES:

K

NAME:

SITE:

USERNAME:

PASSWORD:

NOTES:

NAME:

SITE:

USERNAME:

PASSWORD:

NOTES:

NAME:

SITE:

USERNAME:

PASSWORD:

NOTES:

K

NAME:

SITE:

USERNAME:

PASSWORD:

NOTES:

NAME:

SITE:

USERNAME:

PASSWORD:

NOTES:

NAME:

SITE:

USERNAME:

PASSWORD:

NOTES:

L

NAME:

SITE:

USERNAME:

PASSWORD:

NOTES:

NAME:

SITE:

USERNAME:

PASSWORD:

NOTES:

NAME:

SITE:

USERNAME:

PASSWORD:

NOTES:

L

NAME:

SITE:

USERNAME:

PASSWORD:

NOTES:

NAME:

SITE:

USERNAME:

PASSWORD:

NOTES:

NAME:

SITE:

USERNAME:

PASSWORD:

NOTES:

L

NAME:

SITE:

USERNAME:

PASSWORD:

NOTES:

NAME:

SITE:

USERNAME:

PASSWORD:

NOTES:

NAME:

SITE:

USERNAME:

PASSWORD:

NOTES:

L

NAME:

SITE:

USERNAME:

PASSWORD:

NOTES:

NAME:

SITE:

USERNAME:

PASSWORD:

NOTES:

NAME:

SITE:

USERNAME:

PASSWORD:

NOTES:

M

NAME:

SITE:

USERNAME:

PASSWORD:

NOTES:

NAME:

SITE:

USERNAME:

PASSWORD:

NOTES:

NAME:

SITE:

USERNAME:

PASSWORD:

NOTES:

M

NAME:

SITE:

USERNAME:

PASSWORD:

NOTES:

NAME:

SITE:

USERNAME:

PASSWORD:

NOTES:

NAME:

SITE:

USERNAME:

PASSWORD:

NOTES:

M

NAME:

SITE:

USERNAME:

PASSWORD:

NOTES:

NAME:

SITE:

USERNAME:

PASSWORD:

NOTES:

NAME:

SITE:

USERNAME:

PASSWORD:

NOTES:

M

NAME:

SITE:

USERNAME:

PASSWORD:

NOTES:

NAME:

SITE:

USERNAME:

PASSWORD:

NOTES:

NAME:

SITE:

USERNAME:

PASSWORD:

NOTES:

N

NAME:

SITE:

USERNAME:

PASSWORD:

NOTES:

NAME:

SITE:

USERNAME:

PASSWORD:

NOTES:

NAME:

SITE:

USERNAME:

PASSWORD:

NOTES:

NAME:

_____

SITE:

_____

USERNAME:

_____

PASSWORD:

_____

NOTES:

_____

_____

NAME:

_____

SITE:

_____

USERNAME:

_____

PASSWORD:

_____

NOTES:

_____

_____

NAME:

_____

SITE:

_____

USERNAME:

_____

PASSWORD:

_____

NOTES:

_____

_____

NAME:

SITE:

USERNAME:

PASSWORD:

NOTES:

NAME:

SITE:

USERNAME:

PASSWORD:

NOTES:

NAME:

SITE:

USERNAME:

PASSWORD:

NOTES:

N

NAME:

SITE:

USERNAME:

PASSWORD:

NOTES:

NAME:

SITE:

USERNAME:

PASSWORD:

NOTES:

NAME:

SITE:

USERNAME:

PASSWORD:

NOTES:

NAME:

SITE:

USERNAME:

PASSWORD:

NOTES:

NAME:

SITE:

USERNAME:

PASSWORD:

NOTES:

NAME:

SITE:

USERNAME:

PASSWORD:

NOTES:

NAME:

SITE:

USERNAME:

PASSWORD:

NOTES:

NAME:

SITE:

USERNAME:

PASSWORD:

NOTES:

NAME:

SITE:

USERNAME:

PASSWORD:

NOTES:

NAME:

SITE:

USERNAME:

PASSWORD:

NOTES:

NAME:

SITE:

USERNAME:

PASSWORD:

NOTES:

NAME:

SITE:

USERNAME:

PASSWORD:

NOTES:

NAME:

SITE:

USERNAME:

PASSWORD:

NOTES:

NAME:

SITE:

USERNAME:

PASSWORD:

NOTES:

NAME:

SITE:

USERNAME:

PASSWORD:

NOTES:

P

NAME:

SITE:

USERNAME:

PASSWORD:

NOTES:

NAME:

SITE:

USERNAME:

PASSWORD:

NOTES:

NAME:

SITE:

USERNAME:

PASSWORD:

NOTES:

P

NAME:

SITE:

USERNAME:

PASSWORD:

NOTES:

NAME:

SITE:

USERNAME:

PASSWORD:

NOTES:

NAME:

SITE:

USERNAME:

PASSWORD:

NOTES:

P

NAME:

SITE:

USERNAME:

PASSWORD:

NOTES:

NAME:

SITE:

USERNAME:

PASSWORD:

NOTES:

NAME:

SITE:

USERNAME:

PASSWORD:

NOTES:

P

NAME:

SITE:

USERNAME:

PASSWORD:

NOTES:

NAME:

SITE:

USERNAME:

PASSWORD:

NOTES:

NAME:

SITE:

USERNAME:

PASSWORD:

NOTES:

Q

NAME:

SITE:

USERNAME:

PASSWORD:

NOTES:

NAME:

SITE:

USERNAME:

PASSWORD:

NOTES:

NAME:

SITE:

USERNAME:

PASSWORD:

NOTES:

Q

NAME:

SITE:

USERNAME:

PASSWORD:

NOTES:

NAME:

SITE:

USERNAME:

PASSWORD:

NOTES:

NAME:

SITE:

USERNAME:

PASSWORD:

NOTES:

Q

NAME:

SITE:

USERNAME:

PASSWORD:

NOTES:

NAME:

SITE:

USERNAME:

PASSWORD:

NOTES:

NAME:

SITE:

USERNAME:

PASSWORD:

NOTES:

Q

NAME:

SITE:

USERNAME:

PASSWORD:

NOTES:

NAME:

SITE:

USERNAME:

PASSWORD:

NOTES:

NAME:

SITE:

USERNAME:

PASSWORD:

NOTES:

R

NAME:

SITE:

USERNAME:

PASSWORD:

NOTES:

NAME:

SITE:

USERNAME:

PASSWORD:

NOTES:

NAME:

SITE:

USERNAME:

PASSWORD:

NOTES:

R

NAME:

SITE:

USERNAME:

PASSWORD:

NOTES:

NAME:

SITE:

USERNAME:

PASSWORD:

NOTES:

NAME:

SITE:

USERNAME:

PASSWORD:

NOTES:

R

NAME:

SITE:

USERNAME:

PASSWORD:

NOTES:

NAME:

SITE:

USERNAME:

PASSWORD:

NOTES:

NAME:

SITE:

USERNAME:

PASSWORD:

NOTES:

NAME: _____

SITE: _____

USERNAME: _____

PASSWORD: _____

NOTES: _____

_____

NAME: _____

SITE: _____

USERNAME: _____

PASSWORD: _____

NOTES: _____

_____

NAME: _____

SITE: _____

USERNAME: _____

PASSWORD: _____

NOTES: _____

_____

S

NAME:

SITE:

USERNAME:

PASSWORD:

NOTES:

NAME:

SITE:

USERNAME:

PASSWORD:

NOTES:

NAME:

SITE:

USERNAME:

PASSWORD:

NOTES:

S

NAME:

SITE:

USERNAME:

PASSWORD:

NOTES:

NAME:

SITE:

USERNAME:

PASSWORD:

NOTES:

NAME:

SITE:

USERNAME:

PASSWORD:

NOTES:

S

NAME:

SITE:

USERNAME:

PASSWORD:

NOTES:

NAME:

SITE:

USERNAME:

PASSWORD:

NOTES:

NAME:

SITE:

USERNAME:

PASSWORD:

NOTES:

S

NAME:

SITE:

USERNAME:

PASSWORD:

NOTES:

NAME:

SITE:

USERNAME:

PASSWORD:

NOTES:

NAME:

SITE:

USERNAME:

PASSWORD:

NOTES:

T

NAME:

SITE:

USERNAME:

PASSWORD:

NOTES:

NAME:

SITE:

USERNAME:

PASSWORD:

NOTES:

NAME:

SITE:

USERNAME:

PASSWORD:

NOTES:

T

NAME:

SITE:

USERNAME:

PASSWORD:

NOTES:

NAME:

SITE:

USERNAME:

PASSWORD:

NOTES:

NAME:

SITE:

USERNAME:

PASSWORD:

NOTES:

T

NAME:

SITE:

USERNAME:

PASSWORD:

NOTES:

NAME:

SITE:

USERNAME:

PASSWORD:

NOTES:

NAME:

SITE:

USERNAME:

PASSWORD:

NOTES:

NAME:

SITE:

USERNAME:

PASSWORD:

NOTES:

NAME:

SITE:

USERNAME:

PASSWORD:

NOTES:

NAME:

SITE:

USERNAME:

PASSWORD:

NOTES:

U

NAME:

SITE:

USERNAME:

PASSWORD:

NOTES:

NAME:

SITE:

USERNAME:

PASSWORD:

NOTES:

NAME:

SITE:

USERNAME:

PASSWORD:

NOTES:

U

NAME:

SITE:

USERNAME:

PASSWORD:

NOTES:

NAME:

SITE:

USERNAME:

PASSWORD:

NOTES:

NAME:

SITE:

USERNAME:

PASSWORD:

NOTES:

U

NAME:

SITE:

USERNAME:

PASSWORD:

NOTES:

NAME:

SITE:

USERNAME:

PASSWORD:

NOTES:

NAME:

SITE:

USERNAME:

PASSWORD:

NOTES:

NAME:

SITE:

USERNAME:

PASSWORD:

NOTES:

NAME:

SITE:

USERNAME:

PASSWORD:

NOTES:

NAME:

SITE:

USERNAME:

PASSWORD:

NOTES:

V

NAME:

SITE:

USERNAME:

PASSWORD:

NOTES:

NAME:

SITE:

USERNAME:

PASSWORD:

NOTES:

NAME:

SITE:

USERNAME:

PASSWORD:

NOTES:

V

NAME:

SITE:

USERNAME:

PASSWORD:

NOTES:

NAME:

SITE:

USERNAME:

PASSWORD:

NOTES:

NAME:

SITE:

USERNAME:

PASSWORD:

NOTES:

V

NAME:

SITE:

USERNAME:

PASSWORD:

NOTES:

NAME:

SITE:

USERNAME:

PASSWORD:

NOTES:

NAME:

SITE:

USERNAME:

PASSWORD:

NOTES:

V

NAME:

SITE:

USERNAME:

PASSWORD:

NOTES:

NAME:

SITE:

USERNAME:

PASSWORD:

NOTES:

NAME:

SITE:

USERNAME:

PASSWORD:

NOTES:

W

NAME:

SITE:

USERNAME:

PASSWORD:

NOTES:

NAME:

SITE:

USERNAME:

PASSWORD:

NOTES:

NAME:

SITE:

USERNAME:

PASSWORD:

NOTES:

W

NAME:

SITE:

USERNAME:

PASSWORD:

NOTES:

NAME:

SITE:

USERNAME:

PASSWORD:

NOTES:

NAME:

SITE:

USERNAME:

PASSWORD:

NOTES:

W

NAME:

SITE:

USERNAME:

PASSWORD:

NOTES:

NAME:

SITE:

USERNAME:

PASSWORD:

NOTES:

NAME:

SITE:

USERNAME:

PASSWORD:

NOTES:

W

NAME:

SITE:

USERNAME:

PASSWORD:

NOTES:

NAME:

SITE:

USERNAME:

PASSWORD:

NOTES:

NAME:

SITE:

USERNAME:

PASSWORD:

NOTES:

X

NAME:

SITE:

USERNAME:

PASSWORD:

NOTES:

NAME:

SITE:

USERNAME:

PASSWORD:

NOTES:

NAME:

SITE:

USERNAME:

PASSWORD:

NOTES:

X

NAME: _____

SITE: _____

USERNAME: _____

PASSWORD: _____

NOTES: _____

_____

NAME: _____

SITE: _____

USERNAME: _____

PASSWORD: _____

NOTES: _____

_____

NAME: _____

SITE: _____

USERNAME: _____

PASSWORD: _____

NOTES: _____

_____

X

NAME:

SITE:

USERNAME:

PASSWORD:

NOTES:

NAME:

SITE:

USERNAME:

PASSWORD:

NOTES:

NAME:

SITE:

USERNAME:

PASSWORD:

NOTES:

X

NAME:

SITE:

USERNAME:

PASSWORD:

NOTES:

NAME:

SITE:

USERNAME:

PASSWORD:

NOTES:

NAME:

SITE:

USERNAME:

PASSWORD:

NOTES:

Y

NAME:

SITE:

USERNAME:

PASSWORD:

NOTES:

NAME:

SITE:

USERNAME:

PASSWORD:

NOTES:

NAME:

SITE:

USERNAME:

PASSWORD:

NOTES:

Y

NAME:

SITE:

USERNAME:

PASSWORD:

NOTES:

NAME:

SITE:

USERNAME:

PASSWORD:

NOTES:

NAME:

SITE:

USERNAME:

PASSWORD:

NOTES:

Y

NAME:

SITE:

USERNAME:

PASSWORD:

NOTES:

NAME:

SITE:

USERNAME:

PASSWORD:

NOTES:

NAME:

SITE:

USERNAME:

PASSWORD:

NOTES:

Y

NAME:

SITE:

USERNAME:

PASSWORD:

NOTES:

NAME:

SITE:

USERNAME:

PASSWORD:

NOTES:

NAME:

SITE:

USERNAME:

PASSWORD:

NOTES:

Z

NAME:

SITE:

USERNAME:

PASSWORD:

NOTES:

NAME:

SITE:

USERNAME:

PASSWORD:

NOTES:

NAME:

SITE:

USERNAME:

PASSWORD:

NOTES:

Z

NAME:

SITE:

USERNAME:

PASSWORD:

NOTES:

NAME:

SITE:

USERNAME:

PASSWORD:

NOTES:

NAME:

SITE:

USERNAME:

PASSWORD:

NOTES:

Z

NAME:

SITE:

USERNAME:

PASSWORD:

NOTES:

NAME:

SITE:

USERNAME:

PASSWORD:

NOTES:

NAME:

SITE:

USERNAME:

PASSWORD:

NOTES:

Z

NAME:

SITE:

USERNAME:

PASSWORD:

NOTES:

NAME:

SITE:

USERNAME:

PASSWORD:

NOTES:

NAME:

SITE:

USERNAME:

PASSWORD:

NOTES:

CONTACTS

NAME:

ADDRESS:

CITY: STATE: ZIP CODE:

HOME PHONE: WORK PHONE:

CELL PHONE:

EMAIL:

NAME:

ADDRESS:

CITY: STATE: ZIP CODE:

HOME PHONE: WORK PHONE:

CELL PHONE:

EMAIL:

NAME:

ADDRESS:

CITY: STATE: ZIP CODE:

HOME PHONE: WORK PHONE:

CELL PHONE:

EMAIL:

NAME:

ADDRESS:

CITY: STATE: ZIP CODE:

HOME PHONE: WORK PHONE:

CELL PHONE:

EMAIL:

NAME:

ADDRESS:

CITY: STATE: ZIP CODE:

HOME PHONE: WORK PHONE:

CELL PHONE:

EMAIL:

NAME:

ADDRESS:

CITY: STATE: ZIP CODE:

HOME PHONE: WORK PHONE:

CELL PHONE:

EMAIL:

CONTACTS

NAME:

ADDRESS:

CITY: STATE: ZIP CODE:

HOME PHONE: WORK PHONE:

CELL PHONE:

EMAIL:

NAME:

ADDRESS:

CITY: STATE: ZIP CODE:

HOME PHONE: WORK PHONE:

CELL PHONE:

EMAIL:

NAME:

ADDRESS:

CITY: STATE: ZIP CODE:

HOME PHONE: WORK PHONE:

CELL PHONE:

EMAIL:

NAME:

ADDRESS:

CITY: STATE: ZIP CODE:

HOME PHONE: WORK PHONE:

CELL PHONE:

EMAIL:

NAME:

ADDRESS:

CITY: STATE: ZIP CODE:

HOME PHONE: WORK PHONE:

CELL PHONE:

EMAIL:

NAME:

ADDRESS:

CITY: STATE: ZIP CODE:

HOME PHONE: WORK PHONE:

CELL PHONE:

EMAIL:

www.ingramcontent.com/pod-product-compliance
Lightning Source LLC
Chambersburg PA
CBHW071259310326
41914CB00109B/692